# In the Year 1993

By

**Kerry Butters.**

# In the Year 1993

**Millennium:**                     **2nd millennium**

**Centuries:**        19th century – **20th century** – 21st century

**Decades:**     1960s  1970s  1980s  – **1990s** –  2000s  2010s  2020s

**Years:**            1990 1991 1992 – **1993** – 1994 1995 1996

**1993 (MCMXCIII)** was a common year starting on Friday (dominical letter C) of the Gregorian calendar, the 1993rd year of the Common Era (CE) and *Anno Domini* (AD) designations, the 993rd year of the 2nd millennium, the 93rd year of the 20th century, and the 4th year of the 1990s decade.

# Contents

# Events

## January

- January 1
  - Czechoslovakia ceases to exist as the Czech Republic and Slovakia separate in the so-called Velvet Divorce.
  - The European Economic Community eliminates trade barriers and creates a European single market.
  - British ITV companies GMTV, Carlton Television, Meridian Broadcasting and Westcountry Television start broadcasting, replacing TV-am, Thames Television, TVS and TSW respectively.
- January 2 – Sri Lankan Civil War: The Sri Lanka Navy kills 35-100 civilians on the Jaffna Lagoon.
- January 3
  - In Moscow, Presidents George H. W. Bush (United States) and Boris Yeltsin (Russia) sign the second Strategic Arms Reduction Treaty.
  - The third *Star Trek* TV series *Deep Space Nine* premieres in syndication.
- January 5
  - The state of Washington executes Westley Allan Dodd by hanging (the first judicial hanging in America since 1965).
  - US$7.4 million is stolen from the Brink's Armored Car Depot in Rochester, New York in the 5th largest robbery in U.S. history. Four men, Samuel Millar, Father Patrick Moloney, former Rochester Police officer Thomas O'Connor, and

Charles McCormick, all of whom have ties to the Provisional Irish Republican Army, are accused.
- MV *Braer*, a Liberian-registered oil tanker, runs aground off the Scottish island of Mainland, Shetland, causing a massive oil spill.
- January 6 – Douglas Hurd is the first high-ranking British official to visit Argentina since the Falklands War.
- January 6–20 – The Bombay Riots take place in Mumbai.
- January 7 – The Fourth Republic of Ghana is inaugurated, with Jerry Rawlings as president.
- January 8–17 – The Braer Storm of January 1993, the most intense extratropical cyclone on record for the northern Atlantic Ocean, occurs.
- January 11 – *Monday Night Raw*, the longest running weekly episodic show of the World Wrestling Entertainment/Federation (WWE/F), debuts on television in the United States.
- January 14 – The Polish ferry MS *Jan Heweliusz* sinks off the coast of Rügen in the Baltic Sea, killing 54 people.
- January 15 – Salvatore Riina, the Mafia boss known as 'The Beast', is arrested in Palermo, Sicily, after 23 years as a fugitive.
- January 19
  - The Chemical Weapons Convention (CWC) is signed.
  - IBM announces a $4.97 billion loss for 1992, the largest single-year corporate loss in United States history to date.
  - Iraq disarmament crisis: Iraq refuses to allow UNSCOM inspectors to use its own aircraft to fly into Iraq, and begins military operations in the demilitarized zone between Iraq and Kuwait, and the northern Iraqi no-fly zones. U.S. forces fire approximately 40 Tomahawk cruise missiles at Baghdad factories linked to Iraq's illegal nuclear weapons program. Iraq then informs UNSCOM that it will be able to resume its flights.
- January 20 – Bill Clinton succeeds George H. W. Bush as the 42nd President of the United States.
- January 24 – In Turkey, thousands protest the murder of journalist Uğur Mumcu.

- January 25
  - Mir Aimal Kasi fires a rifle and kills two employees outside Central Intelligence Agency headquarters in Langley, Virginia.
  - Social Democrat Poul Nyrup Rasmussen succeeds Conservative Poul Schlüter as Prime Minister of Denmark.
  - The Russian space station Mir boasts the first art exhibition in outer space.
- January 26 – Václav Havel is elected President of the Czech Republic.

**February**

**The aftermath of the World Trade Center bombing.**

- February 4 – Members of the right-wing Austrian Freedom Party of Austria split to form the Liberal Forum in protest against the increasing nationalistic bent of the party.
- February 5 – Belgium becomes a federal monarchy rather than a unitary kingdom.
- February 8 – General Motors sues NBC, after *Dateline NBC* allegedly rigged 2 crashes showing that some GM pickups can easily catch fire if hit in certain places. NBC settles the lawsuit the following day.
- February 10
  - Lien Chan is named by Lee Teng-hui to succeed Hau Pei-tsun as Premier of the Republic of China.
  - Mani pulite scandal: Italian legislator Claudio Martelli resigns, followed by various politicians over the next 2 weeks.
- February 11 – Janet Reno is selected by President Clinton as Attorney General of the United States.

- February 12 – Two-year-old James Bulger is abducted from New Strand Shopping Centre by two ten-year-old boys, who later torture and murder him.
- February 14
    - Glafcos Clerides defeats incumbent George Vasiliou in the Cypriot presidential election.
    - Albert Zafy defeats Didier Ratsiraka in the Madagascar presidential election.
- February 17 – A ferry sinks in Haiti, killing approximately 1,215 out of 1,500 passengers.
- February 21 – *Star Fox* (series) is released, marking the first 3D Polygonal Star Fox title for the Super Famicom/Super Nintendo Entertainment System smash hit game developed by Nintendo with programming assistance by Argonaut Software (currently Argonaut Games).
- February 22 – UN Security Council Resolution 808 is voted on, deciding that "an international tribunal shall be established" to prosecute violations of international law in Yugoslavia. The tribunal is established on May 25 by Resolution 827.
- February 24 – Prime Minister of Canada Brian Mulroney resigns amidst political and economic turmoil. Kim Campbell, his successor, becomes Canada's first female Prime Minister.
- February 26 – World Trade Center bombing: In New York City, a van bomb parked below the North Tower of the World Trade Center explodes, killing 6 and injuring over 1,000.
- February 28 – Bureau of Alcohol, Tobacco, Firearms and Explosives agents raid the Branch Davidian compound in Waco, Texas, with a warrant to arrest leader David Koresh on federal firearms violations. Four agents and five Davidians die in the raid and a 51-day standoff begins.

## March

- March 4 – Authorities announce the capture of suspected World Trade Center bombing conspirator Mohammad Salameh.

- March 5 – Macedonian Palair Flight 305, a F-100 on a flight to Zürich, crashes shortly after take-off from Skopje, killing 83 of the 97 on board.
- March 8 – The Moon moves into its nearest point to Earth, called perigee, at the same time as its fullest phase of the Lunar Cycle. The Moon appears to be 14% bigger and 30% brighter than the year's other full moons. The next time these two events coincided was in 2008.
- March 11 – Janet Reno is confirmed by the United States Senate and sworn in the next day, becoming the first female Attorney General of the United States.
- March 12
  - 1993 Bombay bombings: Several bombs explode in Bombay, India, killing 257 and injuring hundreds more.
  - North Korea nuclear weapons program: North Korea announces that it plans to withdraw from the Nuclear Nonproliferation Treaty and refuses to allow inspectors access to nuclear sites.
- March 13–March 15 – The Great Blizzard of 1993 strikes the eastern U.S., bringing record snowfall and other severe weather all the way from Cuba to Quebec; it reportedly kills 184.
- March 13 – Australian federal election, 1993: The Australian Labor Party stays in power despite poor economic results.
- March 17 – The Kurdistan Workers' Party announces a unilateral ceasefire in Iraq.
- March 20 – Warrington bomb attacks: A Provisional Irish Republican Army bomb explodes in Warrington Town Centre and kills 2 children, Jonathan Ball and Tim Parry.
- March 22 – The Intel Corporation ships the first P5 Pentium chips.
- March 24
  - The Israeli Knesset elects Ezer Weizman as President of Israel.
  - South Africa officially abandons its nuclear weapons programme. President de Klerk announces that the country's 6 warheads had already been dismantled in 1989.
- March 27

- Jiang Zemin becomes President of the People's Republic of China.
  - Following a rash of integrist murders, Algeria breaks diplomatic relations with Iran, accusing the country of interfering in its interior affairs.
  - Mahamane Ousmane is elected president of Niger.
- March 28 – French legislative election, 1993: Rally for the Republic (Gaullist party) wins a majority and Édouard Balladur becomes Prime Minister.
- March 29 – The 65th Academy Awards, hosted by Billy Crystal, are held at the Dorothy Chandler Pavilion in Los Angeles, with *Unforgiven* winning Best Picture.

## April

- April – The Kuwaiti government claims to uncover an Iraqi assassination plot against former U.S. President George Bush shortly after his visit to Kuwait. Two Iraqi nationals confess to driving a car-bomb into Kuwait on behalf of the Iraqi Intelligence Service.
- April 1 – The Vatican orders the moving of the Carmelite convent at Auschwitz.
- April 6 – A nuclear accident occurs at Tomsk 7 in Russia.
- April 8 – The Republic of Macedonia is admitted to the United Nations.
- April 10 – African National Congress activist Chris Hani is assassinated in South Africa.
- April 16 – Bosnian War: the enclave of Srebrenica is declared a UN-protected "safe area".
- April 19
  - A 51-day stand-off at the Branch Davidian compound near Waco, Texas, ends with a fire that kills 76 people, including David Koresh.
  - South Dakota governor George Mickelson and 7 others are killed when a state-owned aircraft crashes near Dubuque, Iowa.

- April 21 – The Supreme Court in La Paz, Bolivia, sentences former dictator Luis Garcia Meza to 30 years in jail without parole for murder, theft, fraud and violating the constitution.
- April 22 – In Washington, D.C., the Holocaust Memorial Museum is dedicated.
- April 23
  - The World Health Organization declares tuberculosis a Global Emergency.
  - Eritreans vote overwhelmingly for independence from Ethiopia in a United Nations-monitored referendum, the Eritrean independence referendum.
- April 24 – A huge IRA truck bomb explodes at Bishopsgate in the centre of London's financial district, killing one person and causing extensive damage to the area.
- April 26 – Oscar Luigi Scalfaro appoints Carlo Azeglio Ciampi as Prime Minister of Italy.
- April 27
  - Eritrea: Eritrean independence is declared as a result of a referendum held with United Nations verification.
  - Yemeni parliamentary election, 1993: The General People's Congress wins a plurality of 121 seats.
  - All members of the Zambia national football team die in a plane crash off Libreville, Gabon en route to Dakar, Senegal.
- April 28 – An executive order requires the United States Air Force to allow women to fly war planes.
- April 30 – Tennis star Monica Seles is stabbed in the back by an obsessed fan of rival Steffi Graf at a tournament in Hamburg, Germany.

## May

- May 1
  - Pierre Bérégovoy, former Prime Minister of France, commits suicide.
  - A Tamil Tigers suicide bomber assassinates President Ranasinghe Premadasa of Sri Lanka.

- o Dingiri Banda Wijetunga became third executive president of Sri Lanka.
- May 4 – UNOSOM II assumes the Somalian duties of the dissolved UNITAF.
- May 9 – Juan Carlos Wasmosy becomes the first democratically elected President of Paraguay in nearly 40 years.
- May 15 – Niamh Kavanagh wins the Eurovision Song Contest for Ireland with "In Your Eyes".
- May 16 – The Grand National Assembly of Turkey elects Prime Minister Süleyman Demirel as President of Turkey. After Demirel becomes president, the acting Prime Minister of Turkey is Erdal İnönü of Social Democratic Populist Party for 40 days.
- May 24 – Eritrea gains independence from Ethiopia.
- May 25 – The International Criminal Tribunal for the former Yugoslavia is created in The Hague.
- May 27 – Massacre of Via dei Georgofili: A car bomb planted outside the Uffizi Gallery in Florence by the Mafia kills 5 and irretrievably destroys 3 paintings.
- May 28
  - o Eritrea and Monaco gain entry to the United Nations.
  - o *Super Mario Bros.*, the first major American movie based on a video game, is released in theaters.
- May 29 – The first Life Ball takes place in Vienna, Austria. In 2011, the event is named the largest public charity on HIV and AIDS in Europe.

## June

- June 1
  - o Large protests erupt against Slobodan Milošević's regime in Belgrade; opposition leader Vuk Drašković and his wife Danica are arrested.
  - o President of Guatemala Jorge Serrano Elías is forced to flee the country after an attempted self-coup.
  - o Burundian presidential election, 1993: The first multiparty elections in Burundi since the country's independence lead to

the election of Melchior Ndadaye, leader of the Front for Democracy in Burundi. The next day's legislative election sees his party win with an overwhelming majority.

- June 5
  - The National Assembly of Venezuela designates Ramón José Velásquez as successor of suspended President Carlos Andrés Pérez.
  - 24 Pakistani troops in the United Nations forces are killed in Mogadishu, Somalia.
- June 6
  - Following the Revolutionary Nationalist Movement's victory, Gonzalo Sánchez de Lozada becomes president of Bolivia.
  - Mongolia holds its first direct presidential elections.
- June 8 – The PKK-declared ceasefire ends in Iraq.
- June 14 – Multipartyists win a referendum on the future of the one-party system in Malawi.
- June 18 – Iraq disarmament crisis: Iraq refuses to allow UNSCOM weapons inspectors to install remote-controlled monitoring cameras at two missile engine test stands.
- June 20 – John Paxson's 3-point shot in game six of the NBA Finals helps the Chicago Bulls secure a 99–98 win over the Phoenix Suns, and their third consecutive championship.
- June 22 – Japan's New Party Sakigake breaks away from the Liberal Democratic Party.
- June 23 – In Manassas, Virginia, Lorena Bobbitt cuts off the penis of her husband John Wayne Bobbitt.
- June 24
  - A Unabomber bomb injures computer scientist David Gelernter at Yale University.
  - Andrew Wiles wins worldwide fame after presenting his proof of Fermat's Last Theorem, a problem that had been unsolved for more than three centuries.
- June 25
  - Kim Campbell becomes the 19th, and first female, Prime Minister of Canada.

- Tansu Çiller of True Path Party forms the new government of Turkey.
  - Zoran Lilić succeeds Dobrica Ćosić as President of Yugoslavia.
  - The litas is introduced in Lithuania.
  - Jacques Attali resigns as President of the European Bank for Reconstruction and Development.
- June 26–June 28 – Typhoon Koryn causes massive damage to the Philippines, China and Macau.
- June 27
  - U.S. President Bill Clinton orders a cruise missile attack on Iraqi intelligence headquarters in the Al-Mansur District of Baghdad, in response to an Iraqi plot to assassinate former U.S. President George H. W. Bush during his visit to Kuwait in mid-April.
  - In Bad Kleinen, Germany, GSG 9 troopers arrest Birgit Hogefeld and kill Wolfgang Grams, two Red Army Faction terrorists.

## July

- July 2
  - An integrist mob sets fire to the hotel where *The Satanic Verses* translator Aziz Nesin resides in Sivas, Turkey, killing 37.
  - 266 people died after a floating chapel, sank in Bocaue, Bulacan.
- July 5
  - Iraq disarmament crisis: UN inspection teams leave Iraq. Iraq then agrees to UNSCOM demands and the inspection teams return.
  - Electrochemist Faiza Al-Kharafi is appointed rector (president) of Kuwait University, the first woman to head a major university in the Middle East.
- July 7–July 9 – The 19th G7 summit is held in Tokyo, Japan.

- July 7 – Hurricane Calvin lands in Mexico. It is the second Pacific hurricane on record to land in Mexico in July, and kills 34.
- July 12 – A magnitude 7.8 earthquake off Hokkaidō, Japan launches a devastating tsunami that kills 202 on the small island of Okushiri, Hokkaido.
- July 16–17 – In Estonia, the majority Russian cities of Narva and Sillamäe organize illegal referendums on "territorial autonomy" to protest new citizenship laws.
- July 19
  - Japanese general election, 1993: The loss of majority of the Liberal Democratic Party results in a coalition taking power.
  - U.S. President Bill Clinton announces his 'Don't ask, don't tell' policy regarding gays in the American military.
- July 20 – White House deputy counsel Vince Foster commits suicide in Virginia.
- July 23 – Candelária massacre: Brazilian police officers kill eight street kids in Rio de Janeiro.
- July 26
  - Miguel Indurain wins the 1993 Tour de France.
  - Asiana Airlines Flight 733 crashes into Mt. Ungeo in Haenam, South Korea; 68 die.
- July 27 – Windows NT 3.1, the first version of Microsoft's line of Windows NT operating systems, is released to manufacturing.
- July 29 – The Israeli Supreme Court acquits accused Nazi death camp guard John Demjanjuk of all charges and he is set free.

## August

- August 4
  - A federal judge sentences Los Angeles Police Department officers Stacey Koon and Laurence Powell to 30 months in prison for violating motorist Rodney King's civil rights.
  - The Japanese government issues the Kono Statement, acknowledging the comfort women's (sex slaves) deportation.
  -

- August 5
  - The discovery of the Tel Dan Stele, the first archaeological confirmation of the existence of the Davidic line, is announced.
  - Magic: The Gathering undergoes its first general release.
- August 6 – According to Japanese government and TBS networks reports, torrential rain and mudslides kill 72 in Kagoshima, Japan.
- August 9 – King Albert II of Belgium is sworn into office nine days after the death of his brother, King Baudouin I.
- August 13 – Over 130 die in the collapse of Royal Plaza Hotel at Nakhon Ratchasima in Thailand's worst hotel disaster.
- August 16 – Debian announced, initially called "the Debian Linux Release".
- August 17 – For the first time, the public is allowed inside Buckingham Palace in London.
- August 18 – The 14th century Kapellbrücke covered wooden truss bridge in Lucerne (Switzerland) is largely destroyed by fire.
- August 21 – NASA loses radio contact with the Mars Observer orbiter 3 days before the spacecraft is scheduled to enter orbit around Mars.
- August 28 – Ong Teng Cheong becomes the first President of Singapore elected by the population.
- August 28 – *Mighty Morphin Power Rangers*, one of the longest running and most popular science fiction franchises, debuts on Fox Kids with the episode Day of the Dumpster.
- August 31 – Russia completes removing its troops from Lithuania.

# September

**PLO leader Yasir Arafat and Israeli prime minister Yitzhak Rabin, with US President, Bill Clinton.**

- September 13
    - Norwegian parliamentary election, 1993: The Labour Party wins a plurality of the seats, and Prime Minister Gro Harlem Brundtland retains office.
    - Oslo I Accord: PLO leader Yasser Arafat and Israeli prime minister Yitzhak Rabin shake hands in Washington, D.C., after signing a peace accord.
- September 15 – Giuseppe 'Pino' Puglisi, an Italian priest in the Palermo neighborhood of Brancaccio, is assassinated in front of his church on his 56th birthday in retaliation for his anti-Mafia activism. One of the hitmen later confessed that Fr. Puglisi's last words as his killers approached were: "I've been expecting you."
- September 15–September 21 – Hurricane Gert crosses from the Atlantic to the Pacific Ocean through Central America and Mexico.
- September 17 – Russian troops withdraw from Poland.
- September 19 – Polish parliamentary election, 1993: A coalition of the Democratic Left Alliance and the Polish People's Party led by Waldemar Pawlak comes into power.
- September 22 – Big Bayou Canot train disaster: A bridge collapses as the *Sunset Limited* crosses it, killing 47.
- September 23 – The International Olympic Committee selects Sydney, Australia to host the 2000 Summer Olympics.

- September 24 – The Cambodian monarchy is restored, with Norodom Sihanouk as king.
- September 26
    - The first mission in Biosphere 2 ends after two years.
    - PoSAT-1 (the first Portuguese satellite) is launched on board French rocket Ariane 4.
- September 27 – War in Abkhazia – Fall of Sukhumi: Eduard Shevardnadze accuses Russia of passive complicity.
- September 30 – The 6.2 Mw Latur earthquake shakes Maharashtra, India with a maximum Mercalli intensity of VIII (*Severe*) killing 9,748 and injuring 30,000.

## October

- October 3 – Battle of Mogadishu: The U.S. Army conducts Operation Gothic Serpent in the city of Mogadishu, Somalia, using Task Force Ranger. Two UH-60 Blackhawks are shot down and the operation leaves over 1,000 Somalians dead and over 73 Americans WIA, 18 KIA, and 1 captured.
- October 4 – The Russian constitutional crisis culminates with Russian military and security forces clearing the White House of Russia Parliament building by force, quashing a mass uprising against President Boris Yeltsin.
- October 5
    - China performs a nuclear test, ending a worldwide *de facto* moratorium.
    - The papal encyclical *Veritatis Splendor* is promulgated.
- October 10 – The South Korean ferry *Seohae* capsizes off Pusan, South Korea; 292 are killed.
- October 11–October 28 – The UNMIH is prevented from entering Haiti. On October 18, economic sanctions (abolished in August) are reinstated.
- October 13
    - Greek legislative election, 1993: Andreas Papandreou begins his second term as Prime Minister of Greece.
    - The fifth summit of the Francophonie opens in Mauritius.

- October 19 – Benazir Bhutto becomes the Prime Minister of Pakistan for the second time.
- October 21 – A coup in Burundi results in the death of president Melchior Ndadaye and sparks the Burundi Civil War.
- October 25 – Canadian federal election, 1993: Jean Chrétien and his Liberal Party defeat the governing Progressive Conservative Party, which falls to a historic low of 2 seats.
- October 30 – Greysteel massacre: Three members of the Ulster Defence Association, a loyalist paramilitary group, attack a crowded bar in Greysteel, Northern Ireland, with firearms, killing 8 civilians and wounding 13. The bar was targeted because it is in an Irish nationalist and Catholic area.

## November

- November 1 – The Maastricht Treaty takes effect, formally establishing the European Union.
- November 5 – The Parliament of the United Kingdom passes the Railways Act 1993, setting out the procedures for privatisation of British Rail.
- November 9 – Bosnian Croat forces destroy the *Stari Most*, or Old Bridge of Mostar, Bosnia and Herzegovina, by tank fire.
- November 11
  - Microsoft releases Windows for Workgroups 3.11 to manufacturing.
  - Sri Lankan Civil War – Battle of Pooneryn: Over 400 Sri Lankan military are killed.
- November 12 – London Convention: Marine dumping of radioactive waste is outlawed.
- November 17–November 22 – The North American Free Trade Agreement (NAFTA) passes the legislative houses in the United States, Canada and Mexico.
- November 18
  - In a status referendum, Puerto Rico residents vote with a slim margin to maintain Commonwealth status.

- In South Africa, 21 political parties approve a new constitution.
  - The first meeting of the Asia-Pacific Economic Cooperation summit opens in Seattle.
- November 20
  - Savings and loan crisis: The United States Senate Ethics Committee issues a stern censure of California senator Alan Cranston for his dealings with savings-and-loan executive Charles Keating.
  - An Avioimpex Yakovlev Yak-42D crashes into Mount Trojani near Ohrid, Macedonia. The aircraft was on a flight from Geneva, Switzerland to Skopje, but had been diverted to Ohrid due to poor weather conditions at the Skopje airport. All 8 crew members and 115 of the 116 passengers are killed.
- November 28 – *The Observer* reveals that a channel of communications has existed between the Provisional Irish Republican Army and the British government, despite the government's persistent denials.
- November 30 – An agreement establishing the Permanent Commission for East African Co-operation is signed. U.S. President Bill Clinton signs the Brady Handgun Violence Prevention Act

### December

- December 1 – A train crash at Tattenham Corner railway station leads to the introduction of the current drugs and alcohol policy for railways in the UK.
- December 2
  - *STS-61*: NASA launches the Space Shuttle *Endeavour* on a mission to repair an optical flaw in the Hubble Space Telescope.
  - The September 6 merger between Renault and Volvo fails; Volvo CEO Pehr G. Gyllenhammar resigns.

- December 5 – Rafael Caldera Rodríguez is elected President of Venezuela for the second time, succeeding interim president Ramón José Velásquez.
- December 7
  - Colin Ferguson opens fire with his Ruger 9 mm pistol on a Long Island Rail Road train, killing 6 and injuring 19.
  - The 32-member Transitional Executive Committee holds its first meeting in Cape Town, marking the first meeting of an official government body in South Africa with Black members.
  - President of Ivory Coast Félix Houphouët-Boigny dies at 88, the oldest African head of state. He is succeeded three days later by Henri Konan Bédié.
- December 8 – U.S. President Bill Clinton signs into law the North American Free Trade Agreement.
- December 10 – id Software releases *Doom*, a seminal first-person shooter that uses advanced 3D graphics for computer games.
- December 11
  - Chilean presidential election, 1993: Eduardo Frei Ruiz-Tagle is elected with 58% of the vote.
  - A variety of Soviet space program paraphernalia are put to auction in Sotheby's New York, and sell for a total of US$6.8M. One of the items is Lunokhod 1 and its spacecraft Luna 17; they sell for $68,500.
  - One of the three blocks of the Highland Towers near Kuala Lumpur, Malaysia comes down, killing 48.
- December 12 – Péter Boross becomes Prime Minister of Hungary following the death of József Antall.
- December 13
  - Prime Minister of Canada Kim Campbell resigns as leader of the Progressive Conservative Party, and is succeeded as leader by Jean Charest.
  - The Majilis of Kazakhstan approves the nuclear Non-Proliferation Treaty, and agrees to dismantle the more than 100 missiles left on its territory by the fall of the USSR.
- December 15

- ○ Downing Street Declaration: The United Kingdom commits itself to the search for an answer to the problems of Northern Ireland.
  - ○ The Uruguay Round of General Agreement on Tariffs and Trade (GATT) talks reach a successful conclusion after seven years.
  - ○ *Schindler's List*, directed by Steven Spielberg is released in theatres.
- December 16 – Brazil's Supreme Court rules that former President Fernando Collor de Mello may not hold elected office again until 2000 due to political corruption.
- December 18 – Omar Bongo is re-elected as President of Gabon in the country's first multiparty elections.
- December 20
  - ○ The United Nations General Assembly votes unanimously to appoint a U.N. High Commissioner for Human Rights.
  - ○ The first corrected images from the Hubble Telescope are taken.
- December 22 – The interim South African constitution is approved by Parliament 237–45.
- December 29 – Argentina passes a measure allowing President Carlos Menem and all future presidents to run for a second term. It also shortens presidential terms to 4 years and removes the requirement for the president to be Roman Catholic.
- December 30
  - ○ Israel and the Vatican establish diplomatic relations.
  - ○ The Congress Party gains a parliamentary majority in India after the defection of 10 Janata Dal party lawmakers.

### Date unknown

- The second World Parliament of Religions is held in Chicago.
- U.S. President Bill Clinton sends 6 American warships to Haiti, to enforce United Nations trade sanctions against the military-led regime in that country.

- The Mississippi and Missouri Rivers flood large portions of the American Midwest.
- Severe floods hit South Asia, killing over 4,000 people in Bangladesh, India and Nepal.
- The European Exchange Rate Mechanism is put in crisis, mainly from speculation against the French franc.
- Over a dozen people are killed by the new Hantavirus cardiopulmonary syndrome, mainly in the Southwestern United States.
- Wildfires in California destroy over 16,000 acres (65 km$^2$) and 700 homes.
- Stephen Hawking's *A Brief History of Time* becomes the longest-running book on the bestseller list of *The Sunday Times* ever.
- The Oslo Accords negotiations begin.
- Many foreigners are murdered by rebel groups in Algeria.
- The Campaign for Homosexual Law Reform succeeds in having the Irish sodomy law reformed.
- The Jack in the Box E.coli Incident occurred in 1993 when 732 people were infected with the Escherichia coli O157:H7 bacterium originating from undercooked beef patties in hamburgers.
- The genus Prosansanosmilus was discovered and classified with its type species, Prosansanosmilus peregrinus.
- The DFA-2 gene was discovered.

# Births

## January

Aminata Savadogo

Zayn Malik

Paulina Vega

- January 1
  - Alengot Oromait, Ugandan MP
  - Jon Flanagan, English footballer

- January 2 – Bryson Tiller, American singer-songwriter
- January 4
  - Aaryn Doyle, Canadian actress and singer
  - Scott Redding, English Grand Prix motorcycle racer
- January 9
  - Ashley Argota, American actress
  - Aminata Savadogo, Latvian singer and songwriter
- January 11 – Flora Cross, French-American actress
- January 12
  - D.O., South Korean singer (EXO)
  - Aika Mitsui, Japanese singer
  - Zayn Malik, former member of One Direction
- January 13 – Sachika Misawa, Japanese voice actress and singer
- January 14 – Daniel Bessa, Italian-Brazilian footballer
- January 15 – Paulina Vega, Colombian actress, TV Host, model and beauty queen
- January 18 – Morgan York, American actress
- January 19 – Bence Biczó, Hungarian swimmer
- January 22 – Rio Haryanto, Indonesian racing driver
- January 25
  - Charlene Almarvez, Filipina model
  - Kylie Padilla, Australian-Filipina actress
- January 26 – Cameron Bright, Canadian actor
- January 28 – Will Poulter, English actor
- January 29 – Kyary Pamyu Pamyu, Japanese model, blogger, and recording artist

# February

Victoria Justice

Emmelie de Forest

- February 3
  - Getter Jaani, Estonian singer
  - Mishon Ratliff, American singer and actor
- February 5 – Gerard Bieszczad, Polish footballer
- February 6 – Tinashe, American actress and singer
- February 7 – David Dorfman, American actor
- February 9 – Parimarjan Negi, Indian chess prodigy
- February 12
  - Benik Afobe, English footballer
  - Rafinha, Brazilian football player
  - Jennifer Stone, American actress
  - Kana Yume, Japanese gravure idol, actress and AV idol
- February 14 – Shane Harper, American actor and singer
-

- February 17
  - AJ Perez, Filipino actor (d. 2011)
  - Marc Márquez, Spanish Grand Prix motorcycle racer
  - Philip Wiegratz, German actor
- February 19
  - Patrick Johnson, American actor
  - Victoria Justice, American actress and singer
- February 23 – Kasumi Ishikawa, Japanese table tennis player
- February 26 – Taylor Dooley, American actress
- February 27 – Jessica Korda, American golfer
- February 28 – Emmelie de Forest, Danish singer, Eurovision Song Contest 2013 winner

**March**

Josh McEachran

Alia Bhatt

- March 1 – Josh McEachran, English footballer

- March 2 – Mariya Yaremchuk, Ukrainian pop singer
- March 4 – Bobbi Kristina Brown, American singer (d. 2015)
- March 5
  - Bregje Heinen, Dutch model
  - Anna Orlik, Belarusian tennis player
- March 10 – Jeffrey Scaperrotta, American actor
- March 11
  - Anthony Davis, American basketball player
  - Demi Harman, Australian actress
  - Daisuke Ssegwanyi, Ugandan swimmer
- March 14 – Anna Ewers, German model
- March 15
  - Alia Bhatt, British-born Indian actress and singer
  - Alyssa Reid, Canadian singer/songwriter
- March 17 – Julia Winter, Swedish-born English actress
- March 22 – Natalia Starr, Polish pornographic actress
- March 23 – Lee Hyun-woo, South Korean actor
- March 24
  - Grace Cassidy, English actress
  - Ryo Ryusei, Japanese actor
- March 30
  - Anitta, Brazilian singer and dancer
  - Song Min-ho, South Korean rapper (Winner)
- March 31 – Connor Wickham, English footballer

**April**

Daniela Bobadilla

Chance the Rapper

- April 1
    - Blair Fowler, American YouTube beauty guru
    - Keito Okamoto, Japanese singer (Hey! Say! JUMP)
- April 2 – Aaron Kelly, American singer
- April 4 – Daniela Bobadilla, Canadian actress
- April 9 – Will Merrick, English actor
- April 11 – Yuji Takahashi, Japanese footballer
- April 12 – Ryan Nugent-Hopkins, Canadian ice hockey player
- April 13 – Hannah Marks, American actress
- April 14
    - Vivien Cardone, American actress
    - Graham Phillips, American actor and singer
    - Josephine Skriver, Danish model
- April 15 – Madeleine Martin, American television actress/voice actress
- April 16
    - Mirai Nagasu, Japanese-American figure skater
    - Chance the Rapper, American rapper
- April 18 – Nathan Sykes, British singer
- April 19 – Sebastian de Souza, English actor
- April 22
    - Ryu Hwayoung, Korean rapper, dancer, model and actress
    - Ryu Hyoyoung, Korean model, actress and singer
- April 24 – Ben Davies, Welsh footballer
- April 25
    - Alex Bowman, American race car driver

- o Shiloh, Canadian singer-songwriter
- April 27 – Danielle Doty, American beauty pageant titleholder

## May

Kayla Williams

Caroline Zhang

- May 2
  - o Isyana Sarasvati, Indonesian singer
  - o Tao, South Korean singer (EXO)
- May 6 – Naomi Scott, English actress, singer and musician
- May 8 &ndasn; Kayla Williams (gymnast), American gymnast
- May 9
  - o Bonnie Rotten, American pornographic actress and model
  - o Ryosuke Yamada, Japanese actor and singer
- May 10
  - o Halston Sage, American actress
  - o Mirai Shida, Japanese actress

- May 11
  - Maurice Harkless, American-Puerto Rican basketball player
- May 13
  - Finn Harries, English vlogger, designer and entrepreneur
  - Debby Ryan, American actress
  - Romelu Lukaku, Belgian football player
  - Minah, South Korean singer (Girl's Day)
- May 14 – Miranda Cosgrove, American actress and singer
- May 16 – IU, South Korean singer and actress
- May 17 – Ayaka Sayama, Japanese gravure idol
- May 18 – Jessica Watson, Australian sailor
- May 19 – Daisy Mallory, American country singer
- May 20 – Caroline Zhang, American figure skater
- May 28 – Jonnie Peacock, English sprint runner

**June**

George Ezra

Ariana Grande

- June 6 – Frida Gustavsson, Swedish model
- June 7
  - Miro Aaltonen, Finnish professional ice hockey player
  - George Ezra, English singer-songwriter
  - Park Ji-yeon, South Korean singer and actress
- June 10 – Scott McLaughlin, New Zealand racer
- June 15
  - Kanna Arihara, Japanese singer
  - Boone Jenner, Canadian ice hockey player
- June 17 – Jean Marie Froget, Mauritian swimmer
- June 19 – KSIOlajidebt, British YouTuber and rapper
- June 21 – Caroline Brasch Nielsen, Danish model
- June 22
  - Caydee Denney, American pair skater
  - Izzy Miller, American musician
- June 26 – Ariana Grande, American actress and singer
- June 28
  - Bradley Beal, American basketball player
  - Jung Dae-hyun, South Korean singer
- June 29
  - James Sanderson, Gibraltarian swimmer
  - Alyssa Valdez, Filipino Volleyball player

**July**

Cher Lloyd

Alycia Debnam-Carey

- July 1
  - Brett Ritchie, Canadian ice hockey player
  - Raini Rodriguez, American actress
- July 3 – Roy Kim, South Korean singer-songwriter
- July 5
  - Cody Klop, American actor
  - Hollie Cavanagh, British singer
- July 7
  - Ally Brooke, American singer
  - Sam Aston, English actor
  - Capital STEEZ, American Rapper (d. 2012)
- July 9 – Martin Tungevaag, Norwegian DJ
- July 10 – Carlon Jeffery, American actor
- July 11 – Rebecca Bross, American gymnast
- July 18 – Lee Taemin, Korean singer (SHINee)
- July 20 – Alycia Debnam-Carey, Australian actress
- July 22 – Amber Beattie, English Actress
- July 26
  - Taylor Momsen, American actress
  - Elizabeth Gillies, American actress
- July 27
  - Max Power, English footballer
  - Jordan Spieth, American golfer
- July 28
  - Harry Kane, English footballer

- Cher Lloyd, English singer

**August**

Sarah Sjöström

Maia Mitchell

Keke Palmer

- August 1 – Leon Thomas III, American actor and singer
- August 2 – Manika, American singer-songwriter
- August 3 – Yurina Kumai, Japanese singer
- August 4
  - Alan Shirahama, Japanese singer, dancer and actor
  - Saido Berahino; English footballer
- August 5 – Suzuka Ohgo, Japanese child actress
- August 6 – Kaori Ishihara Japanese voice acress
- August 7 – Francesca Eastwood, American actress, model, socialite and television personality
- August 8
  - Ben Breedlove, American Internet personality (d. 2011)
  - Jessie Rogers, Brazilian internet celebrity
- August 10
  - Yuto Nakajima, Japanese singer (Hey! Say! JUMP)
  - Andre Drummond, American basketball player
- August 11
  - Alireza Jahanbakhsh, Iranian footballer
  - Alyson Stoner, American actress, singer, and dancer
- August 12
  - Ewa Farna, Polish singer
  - Luna, South Korean singer and actress
  - Imani Hakim, American actress
- August 13 – Yoon Bo-mi, member of A Pink, South Korea
- August 14 – Cassi Thomson, Australian actress and singer
- August 15 – Alex Oxlade-Chamberlain, English footballer
- August 16 – Cameron Monaghan, American actor
- August 17
  - Yoo Seung-ho, South Korean actor
  - Sarah Sjöström, Swedish record breaking swimmer
  - Madison McReynolds, actress
- August 18
  - Jung Eun-ji, South Korean singer, member of A Pink and actress
  - Maia Mitchell, Australian actress and singer
- August 26 – Keke Palmer, American actress and singer

- August 29
    - Lucas Cruikshank, American actor
    - Liam Payne, member of One Direction
- August 31 – Haruka Imai Japanese figure skater

**September**

Patrick Schwarzenegger

Niall Horan

- September 1
    - Alexander Conti, Canadian actor
    - Ilona Mitrecey, French singer
    - Megan Nicole, American singer-songwriter
    - Silje Norendal, Norwegian snowboarder
- September 2 – Montana Cox, Australian model

- September 5 – Gage Golightly, American actress
- September 9 – Charlie Stewart, American actor
- September 13
  - Aisha Dee, Australian actress
  - Niall Horan, member of One Direction
- September 17 – Alfie Deyes, British vlogger
- September 18 – Patrick Schwarzenegger, American model and actor, son of Arnold Schwarzenegger
- September 20 – Julian Draxler, German footballer
- September 22 – Chase Ellison, American actor
- September 23
  - Pontus Åberg, Swedish ice hockey player
  - Sam Jackson, English actor
- September 26
  - Michael Kidd-Gilchrist, American basketball player
  - Joe Bunney, English footballer
- September 27 – Mónica Puig, Puerto Rican tennis
  - Patrick Mölleken, German actor, dubber and voice-over artist
  - Lisandro Magallán, Argentine professional footballer
  - Vinnie Sunseri, American football player
- September 28 – Jodie Williams, British sprint runner

**October**

Barbara Palvin

Molly Quinn

- October 1 – Christian Bravo, Chilean footballer
- October 2 – Tara Lynne Barr, American actress
- October 4
  - Aidan Mitchell, American actor
  - Ali Brustofski, American singer-songwriter
  - Sam Earle, Canadian actor
- October 6
  - Jourdan Miller, American actress
  - Joe Rafferty, English-born Irish footballer
- October 8
  - Angus T. Jones, American actor
  - Barbara Palvin, Hungarian model and actress
  - Molly Quinn, American actress
  - Garbiñe Muguruza, Spanish professional tennis player
- October 9 – Scotty McCreery, American singer
- October 13 – Tiffany Trump, American socialite
- October 16 – Jovit Baldivino, Filipino singer
- October 20
  - David Bolarinwa, British sprinter
  - Hunter King, American actress
- October 29
  - India Eisley, American actress
  - Sara Jovanović, Serbian singer (Moje 3)

## November

- November 4 – Jordan Smith, American singer, winner of *The Voice* season 9
- November 8 – Lauren Young, Filipino-American model and actress
- November 14 – Luis Gil, American soccer player
- November 16 – Dakota Earnest, American gymnast
- November 17 – Taylor Gold, American Olympian snowboarder
- November 21 – Elena Myers, American racer
- November 24 – Ivi Adamou, Greek Cypriot singer
- November 25 – Danny Kent, English motorcycle racer
- November 26 – Erena Ono, Japanese singer
- November 27 – Aubrey Peeples, American actress and singer
- November 29 – David Lambert, American actor
- November 30 – Yuri Chinen, Japanese singer and actor

## December

Ariadna Gutiérrez

- December 2 – Dylan McLaughlin, American actor
- December 5 – Ross Barkley, English footballer
- December 6
  - Elián González, Cuban refugee
  - Wesley Stromberg, American musician

- December 7 – Jasmine Villegas, American singer
- December 8 – AnnaSophia Robb, American actress
- December 13 – Ryan Cassata, American musician and public speaker
- December 16 – Jyoti Amge, Indian actress
- December 18
  - Ana Porgras, Romanian former gymnast
  - Riria, Japanese actress
- December 19 – Corey Snide, American actor and dancer
- December 22
  - Ali Lohan, American actress, model and singer
  - Meghan Trainor, American singer-songwriter, musician and producer
- December 25
  - Ariadna Gutiérrez, Colombian actress, TV Host, model and beauty queen
  - Emi Takei, Japanese actress, model and singer

# Deaths

## January

Dizzy Gillespie

Rudolf Nureyev

Audrey Hepburn

Hedi Nouira

- January 1
  - Florence Davidson, Canadian First Nations artist (b. 1896)
  - William Ricketts, Australian potter and sculptor (b. 1898)
  - Eddie Arning, farming community of Germania, Texas (b. 1898)
- January 5 – Juan Benet, Spanish writer (b. 1927)
- January 6
  - Dizzy Gillespie, American jazz trumpeter, bandleader, and composer (b. 1917)
  - Richard Mortensen, Danish painter (b. 1910)
  - Rudolf Nureyev, Russian dancer (b. 1938)
- January 9
  - Paul Hasluck, Australian politician, former Governor-General and Cabinet minister (b. 1905)
  - Anton Crihan, Bessarabian politician (b. 1893)
- January 10 – Luther Gulick, expert on public administration (b. 1892)
- January 13 – René Pleven, French politician, former Prime Minister (b. 1901)
- January 15 – Sammy Cahn, American lyricist (b. 1913)
- January 16 – Glenn Corbett, American actor (b. 1930)
- January 18 – Eleanor Burford (Jean Plaidy, Elbur Ford, Kathleen Kellow, Ellalice Tate, Anna Percival, Victoria Holt, Philippa Carr), English writer (b. 1906)

- January 20 – Audrey Hepburn, Belgian-born British-Dutch actress (b. 1929)
- January 21
  - Charlie Gehringer, American baseball player (Detroit Tigers) and member of the MLB Hall of Fame (b. 1903)
  - Leo Löwenthal, German sociologist (b. 1900)
- January 22 – Kōbō Abe, Japanese author (b. 1924)
- January 23 – Thomas A. Dorsey, American musician (b. 1899)
- January 24
  - Gustav Ernesaks, Estonian composer and a choir conductor (b. 1908)
  - Thurgood Marshall, American jurist, First African-American on the Supreme Court (b. 1908)
- January 25 – Hédi Nouira, Tunisian politician, former Prime Minister (b. 1911)
- January 26
  - Baron Axel von dem Bussche, German military officer, member of the anti-Hitler Resistance (b. 1919)
  - Robert Jacobsen Danish artist (b. 1912)
  - Jeanne Sauvé, Canadian politician, former Governor General (b. 1922)
- January 27 – André the Giant, French professional wrestler (b. 1946)
- January 28 – Erik Herseth, Norwegian sailor (b. 1892)
- January 31 – Claude de Cambronne, French aircraft manufacturer (b. 1905)

# February

Ferruccio Lamborghini

Bobby Moore

Lillian Gish

- February 2 – Alexander Schneider, Lithuanian violinist (b. 1908)
- February 3
  - Tan Shaowen, Chinese politician (b. 1929)
  - Karel Goeyvaerts, Belgian composer (b. 1923)
- February 5
  - Hans Jonas, German philosopher (b. 1903)

- Roxanne Kernohan, Canadian actress (b. 1960)
- Tip Tipping, British actor and stuntman (parachuting accident) (b. 1958)
- Joseph L. Mankiewicz, American screenwriter and producer (b. 1909)
- February 6 – Arthur Ashe, American tennis player and civil activist (b. 1943)
- February 8 – Roland Mousnier, French historian (b. 1907)
- February 9
  - Elwood "Pete" Quesada, American air force general (b. 1904)
  - Saburo Okita, former Japanese Foreign Minister (b. 1914)
  - Kate Wilkinson, American stage and television actress (b. 1916)
- February 10 – Maurice Bourgès-Maunoury, French politician, former Prime Minister (b. 1914)
- February 11 – Robert W. Holley, American biochemist, Nobel Prize laureate (b. 1922)
- February 14 – Pedro Cortina y Mauri, Spanish politician, former Foreign Minister (b. 1908)
- February 18 – Kerry Von Erich, American professional wrestler (b. 1960)
- February 20 – Ferruccio Lamborghini, Italian automobile manufacturer (b. 1916)
- February 21
  - Inge Lehmann, Danish seismologist (b. 1888)
  - Dick White, British intelligence officer (b. 1906)
- February 22 – Jean Lecanuet, French politician (b. 1920)
- February 23
  - Phillip Terry, American actor (b. 1909)
  - Robert Triffin, Belgian economist (b. 1911)
- February 24 – Bobby Moore, English footballer (b. 1941)
- February 25
  - Eddie Constantine, American-born French singer and actor (b. 1917)
  - Mary Walter, Filipino actress (b.1912)

- February 26 – Beaumont Newhall, American curator (b. 1908)
- February 27 – Lillian Gish, American actress (b. 1893)
- February 28
  - Ruby Keeler, American actress (b. 1909)
  - Ishirō Honda, Japanese film director (b. 1911)

**March**

Helen Hayes

Polykarp Kusch

Jose Maria Lemus

- March 3
    - Albert Sabin, American biologist, developer of the oral polio vaccine (b. 1906)
    - Carlos Montoya, Spanish flamenco guitarist (b. 1903)
- March 4 – Izaak Kolthoff, American chemist (b. 1894)
- March 5
    - Cyril Collard, French filmmaker (b. 1957)
    - Norman F. Douty, Christian author and pastor (b. 1899)
- March 8 – Billy Eckstine, American musician (b. 1914)
- March 10 – Dino Bravo, Italian-Canadian pro wrestler (b. 1949)
- March 12 – Wang Zhen, Chinese politician, Vice President of the PRC and one of the Eight Elders of the Communist Party of China (b. 1908)
- March 13 – Ann Way, English actress (b. 1915)
- March 15 – Ricardo Arias Espinosa, Panamanian politician, former President of the Republic (b. 1912)
- March 16
    - Muhammad Khan Junejo, Pakistani politician, former Prime Minister (b. 1932)
    - Ralph Fults, last of America's depression-era outlaws (b. 1910)
- March 17 – Helen Hayes, American actress (b. 1900)
- March 20
    - Polykarp Kusch, German-born physicist, Nobel Prize laureate (b. 1911)
    - Paul László, Hungarian-born architect (b. 1900)
- March 24 – John Hersey, American writer and journalist (b. 1914)
- March 26 – Louis Falco, American dancer and choreographer (b. 1942)
- March 27
    - Elizabeth Holloway Marston, American psychologist (b. 1893)
    - Kate Reid, Canadian actress (b. 1930)
    - Kamal Hassan Ali, Egyptian politician, former Prime Minister (b. 1921)
- March 30 – Richard Diebenkorn, American painter (b. 1922)

- March 31
  - Brandon Lee, American actor (b. 1965)
  - José María Lemus, Salvadorean politician and military officer, former President of the Republic (b. 1911)
  - Mitchell Parish, American lyricist (b. 1900)
  - Muriel Morley, English speech therapist (b. 1899)
  - Nicanor Zabaleta, Spanish harpist (b. 1907)

**April**

Marian Anderson

Turgut Özal

- April 1
  - Juan de Borbón y Battenberg, Spanish royal, Count of Barcelona (b. 1913)

- Alan Kulwicki, U.S. race car driver (b. 1954)
- April 2
  - Masaichi Niimi, admiral in the Imperial Japanese Navy during World War II (b. 1887)
  - Eugenie Leontovich, Russian-born actress (b. 1900)
- April 3
  - Peter J. De Muth, Democratic member of the U.S. House of Representatives from Pennsylvania (b. 1892)
  - Pinky Lee, American comedian (b. 1907)
- April 5 – Divya Bharti, Indian actress (b. 1974)
- April 8 – Marian Anderson, American contralto (b. 1897)
- April 10
  - Chris Hani, South African politician (b. 1942)
  - Donald Broadbent, British psychologist (b. 1926)
- April 11 – Rahmon Nabiyev, Tajik politician, former Communist leader and President of the Republic (b. 1930)
- April 12 – George Frederick Ives, last surviving veteran of the Boer Wars (b. 1881)
- April 13
  - Isaac Rojas, Argentinian admiral and statesman (b. 1906)
  - Wallace Stegner, American writer (b. 1909)
- April 15
  - John Tuzo Wilson, Canadian geophysicist and geologist (b. 1908)
  - Leslie Charteris, British author (b. 1907)
  - Robert Westall, British author (b. 1929)
- April 17 – Turgut Özal, Turkish statesman, President of the Republic and former Prime Minister (b. 1927)
- April 20 – Cantinflas, Mexican comedian (b. 1911)
- April 22
  - Stephen Lawrence, British murder victim (b. 1974)
  - Andries Treurnicht, South African politician (b. 1921)
- April 23
  - Guido Carli, Italian politician and economist (b. 1914)
  - Cesar Chavez, Mexican-American civil rights activist (b. 1927)

- April 24 – Oliver Tambo, South African anti-Apartheid politician and former president of the ANC (b. 1911)
- April 25 – Rosita Moreno, Spanish film actress (b. 1907)
- April 26
  - Julia Davis, American educator (b. 1891)
  - Darussalam, Indonesian actor (b. 1920)
- April 29 – Mick Ronson, English rock guitarist (b. 1946)

**May**

- May 1

Pierre Beregovoy

Ranasinghe Premadasa

  - 
  - Pierre Bérégovoy, Prime Minister of France (b. 1925)
  - Ranasinghe Premadasa, Sri Lankan statesman, president of the Republic (assassinated) (b. 1924)
- May 6
  - Ian Mikardo, British labour politician (b. 1908)
  - Ann Todd, English actress (b. 1909)
- May 7
  - Mary Philbin, American actress (b. 1903)

- May 8
  - Avram Davidson, American writer (b. 1923)
  - Alwin Nikolais, American choreographer (b. 1912)
- May 9 – Freya Stark, British explorer and travel writer (b. 1893)
- May 14 – William Randolph Hearst, Jr., American businessman (b. 1908)
- May 22
  - Alfred Vaucher, French theologian, church historian and bibliographer (b. 1887)
  - Mieczysław Horszowski, Polish pianist (b. 1892)
- May 26 – Catherine Caradja, Romanian aristocrat and philanthropist (b. 1893)
- May 30 – Sun Ra, American jazz musician (b. 1914)

**June**

Alexis Smith

James Hunt

William Golding

Pat Nixon

Archie Williams

- June 1 – Austin Robinson, University of Cambridge economist (b. 1897)
- June 2
  - Tahar Djaout, Algerian writer (b. 1954)
  - Johnny Mize, American baseball player (St. Louis Cardinals) and member of the MLB Hall of Fame (b. 1913)
- June 3 – Yeoh Ghim Seng, Singaporean politician, former acting president of the Republic (b. 1918)
- June 5 – Conway Twitty, American musician (b. 1933)
- June 6 – James Bridges, American screenwriter and director (b. 1936)
- June 7 – Dražen Petrović, Croatian basketball Player (b. 1964)
- June 8
  - René Bousquet, head of the Vichy France Police (b. 1909)
  - Severo Sarduy, Cuban poet (b. 1937)
  - Nolan Bailey Harmon, bishop of The Methodist Church and the United Methodist Church (b. 1892)
- June 9 – Alexis Smith, Canadian actress (b. 1921)
- June 10
  - Arleen Auger, American soprano singer (b. 1939)
  - Les Dawson, English Comedian (b. 1931)
  - Milward L. Simpson, American politician (b. 1897)
- June 11
  - Bernard Bresslaw, British actor (b. 1934)
  - Ray Sharkey, American actor (b. 1952)
- June 12
  - Manuel Summers, Spanish film director (b. 1935)
  - Binay Ranjan Sen, Indian diplomat, 4th Director General of the Food and Agriculture Organization (FAO) (b. 1898)
- June 13
  - Deke Slayton, American astronaut (b. 1924)
  - Gérard Côté, Canadian marathon runner (b. 1913)
- June 15
  - John Connally, American politician (b. 1917)
  - James Hunt, British race car driver (b. 1947)
- June 18 – Craig Rodwell, American gay activist (b. 1940)

- June 19
  - William Golding, English writer, Nobel Prize laureate (b. 1911)
  - Szymon Goldberg, Polish-born violinist (b. 1909)
- June 22 – Pat Nixon, First Lady of the United States (b. 1912)
- June 24 – Archie Williams, American athlete (b. 1915)
- June 26 – Roy Campanella, American baseball player (Brooklyn Dodgers) and member of the MLB Hall of Fame (b. 1921)
- June 28 – GG Allin, American punk singer (b. 1956)
- June 29 – Héctor Lavoe, Puerto Rican salsa singer (b. 1946)
- June 30 – Spanky McFarland, American actor (b. 1928)

**July**

Hugo Ballivian

Baudouin of Belgium

- July 2
  - Fred Gwynne, American actor and comedian (b. 1926)
  - Jorge Carpio Nicolle, Guatemalan politician (b. 1932)
  - Edward Dunlop, Australian surgeon (b. 1907)
- July 3
  - Don Drysdale, American baseball player (Los Angeles Dodgers) and member of the MLB Hall of Fame (b. 1936)
  - Joe DeRita, American comedian (b. 1909)
- July 4
  - Anne Shirley, American actress (b. 1918)
  - Lola Gaos, Spanish actress (b. 1921)
- July 5 – Tom Maguire, Irish Republican (b. 1892)
- July 7
  - William McElwee Miller, American missionary to Persia, and author of several books (b. 1892)
  - Mia Zapata, American punk musician (b. 1965)
- July 10 – Masuji Ibuse, Japanese writer (b. 1898)
- July 11 – Mario Bauzá, Cuban musician (b. 1911)
- July 13 – Davey Allison, American stock car driver (b. 1961)
- July 14
  - Léo Ferré, French poet and singer-songwriter (b. 1916)
  - Harold Willmott, South African military commander (b. 1899)
- July 15
  - David Brian, American actor (b. 1914)
  - Hugo Ballivián, Bolivian general, former President of the Republic (b. 1901)
- July 18 – Jean Negulesco, Romanian-born film director (b. 1900)
- July 21 – E. J. G. Pitman, Australian mathematician (b. 1897)
- July 23 – James Jordan, father of basketball superstar, Michael Jordan (b. 1936)
- July 24 – Rene Requiestas, Filipino comedian (b. 1957)
- July 25
  - Nan Grey, American actress (b. 1918)
  - Cecilia Parker, American actress (b. 1914)

- July 26 – Matthew Ridgway, United States Army General (b. 1895)
- July 27 – Reggie Lewis, American basketball player (b. 1965)
- July 30
  - Edward Bernard Raczyński, Polish aristocrat, diplomat, writer, politician and President of Poland (b. 1891)
  - William Guglielmo Niederland, German-American psychoanalyst (b. 1904)
  - Bob Wright, American right-handed professional baseball player (b. 1891)
- July 31
  - Baudouin of Belgium, reigning King of Belgium (b. 1930)
  - Paul B. Henry, American politician (b. 1942)

**August**

Stewart Granger

Kasdi Merbah

- August 1 – Claire Du Brey, American actress (b. 1892)
- August 3
  - James Donald, Scottish actor (b. 1917)
  - Theodore A. Parker III, American ornithologist (b. 1953)
- August 5 – Eugen Suchoň, Slovak composer (b. 1908)

- August 6
  - Genkei Masamune, Japanese botanist (b. 1899)
  - Esad Mekuli, Albanian poet and scholar (b. 1916)
- August 7 – Christopher Gillis, American dancer and choreographer (b. 1951)
- August 10
  - Øystein Aarseth, Norwegian black metal musician (b. 1968)
  - Hendrik G. Stoker, Calvinist philosopher (b. 1899)
  - Irene Sharaff, American costume designer (b. 1910)
- August 16
  - René Dreyfus French Grand Prix racing driver (b. 1905)
  - Stewart Granger, Anglo-American actor (b. 1913)
- August 19 – Salah Jadid, Syrian general and Ba'athist politician (b. 1926)
- August 20 – Bernard Delfgaauw, Dutch philosopher (b. 1912)
- August 21
  - Ichirō Fujiyama, Japanese composer and singer (b. 1911)
  - Kasdi Merbah, Prime Minister of Algeria (b. 1938)
- August 28 – E. P. Thompson, English historian and activist (b. 1924)
- August 30 – Richard Jordan, American actor (b. 1937)

**September**

Raymond Burr

Maurice Yameogo

Jimmy Doolittle

- September 1 – Michael Sobell, British businessman, a major philanthropist, and a prominent owner/breeder of thoroughbred racehorses (b. 1892)
- September 3 – Wesley Englehorn, American football player (b. 1890)
- September 4 – Hervé Villechaize, French-born actor (b. 1943)
- September 7 – Christian Metz, French film theorist (b. 1931)
- September 9 – Helen O'Connell, American singer (b. 1920)
- September 11 – Erich Leinsdorf, Austrian conductor (b. 1912)
- September 12
    - Raymond Burr, Canadian actor (b. 1917)
    - Charles Lamont, Russian-born film director (b. 1895)
- September 13 – Steve Jordan, American jazz guitarist (b. 1919)

- September 15 – Maurice Yaméogo, Burkinabé statesman, first president of late Upper Volta, current Burkina Faso (b. 1921)
- September 20 – Erich Hartmann, German World War II fighter pilot, highest-scoring fighter ace in world history (b. 1922)
- September 22
  - Maurice Abravanel, Greek-born conductor (b. 1903)
  - Regina Fryxell, American composer (b. 1899)
  - Nina Berberova, Russian writer (b. 1901)
- September 24
  - Bruno Pontecorvo, Italian-Soviet nuclear physicist (b.1913)
  - Ian Stuart, singer for white power skinhead band Skrewdriver (b.1957)
- September 25 – John Moores, English businessman and philanthropist (b. 1896)
- September 27 – Jimmy Doolittle, American aviation pioneer and World War II United States Army Air Forces general (b. 1896)
- September 28 – Alexander A. Drabik, American soldier (b. 1910)
- September 29 – Gordon Douglas, American film director (b. 1907)

**October**

Agnes de Mille

Vincent Price

Federico Fellini

- October 5 – Agnes de Mille, American dancer and choreographer (b. 1905)
- October 7 – Cyril Cusack, Irish actor (b. 1910)
- October 12
  - Leon Ames, American actor (b. 1903)
  - Patrick Holt, English actor (b. 1912)
- October 13
  - Otmar Gutmann, German television director. Creator of Pingu (b. 1937).
- October 17 – Criss Oliva, American Musician (b. 1963)
- October 20 – Milan Konjović, prominent Serbian painter (b. 1898)
- October 21
  - James Leo Herlihy, American novelist and playwright (b. 1927)
  - Melchior Ndadaye, President of Burundi (b. 1953)
- October 22
  - Jiří Hájek, Czech politician and diplomat (b. 1913)

- o Said Mohamed Jaffar, former head of State of Comoros (b. 1918)
- October 24 – Jo Grimond, British politician, former leader of the Liberal Party (b. 1913)
- October 25
  - o Vincent Price, American actor (b. 1911)
  - o Danny Chan, Hong Konger singer (b. 1958)
- October 26
  - o Albert Hyzler, Maltese statesman, former acting President (b. 1916)
  - o Harold Rome, American composer (b. 1908)
- October 27/28 – István Rosztóczy, Hungarian microbiologist
- October 28 – Yuri Lotman, Russian formalist critic, semiotician, and culturologist (b. 1922)
- October 29 – Masahiro Makino, Japanese film director (b. 1908)
- October 31
  - o Federico Fellini, Italian film director (b. 1920)
  - o Paul Grégoire, archbishop of Montreal (b. 1911)
  - o River Phoenix, American actor (b. 1970)

**November**

Bill Bixby

Anthony Burgess

- November 1
  - Severo Ochoa, Spanish-born biochemist, recipient of the Nobel Prize in Physiology or Medicine (b. 1905)
  - A. N. Sherwin-White, English historian of Ancient Rome (b. 1911)
- November 3 – Léon Theremin, inventor of the theremin (b. 1896)
- November 6
  - Ralph Randles Stewart, American botanist (b. 1890)
  - Torsten Fenslau, German DJ and record producer (b. 1964)
- November 9
  - Joe "Pegleg" Morgan, senior member of La Eme (b. 1929)
  - Stanley Myers, British film composer (b. 1930)
- November 10
  - Alberto Breccia, Argentine comics artist and writer (b. 1919)
  - Wensley Pithey, South African actor (b. 1914)
- November 12
  - Bill Dickey, American baseball player (New York Yankees) and member of the MLB Hall of Fame (b. 1907)
  - H. R. Haldeman, American political aide and businessman (b. 1926)
  - Anna Sten, Ukrainian-born actress (b. 1908)
- November 14 – Sanzo Nosaka, Japanese Communist politician (b. 1892)
- November 16
  - Achille Zavatta, French circus artist (b. 1915)
  - Lucia Popp, Slovak soprano (b. 1939)
- November 18 – Fritz Feld, German actor (b. 1900)
- November 19 – Leonid Gaidai, Soviet comedy director (b. 1923)
- November 20 – Emile Ardolino, American film director (b. 1943)

- November 21 – Bill Bixby, American actor (b. 1934)
- November 22
  - Anthony Burgess, English author (b. 1917)
  - Joseph Yodoyman, Chadian politician, former Prime Minister (b. 1950)
- November 26 – Eric McKay, Co-operative Commonwealth Federation member (b. 1899)
- November 27 – Rudolph Bierwirth, career officer in the Australian Army (b. 1899)
- November 28
  - Kenneth Connor English comedian (b. 1916)
  - Garry Moore, American television host and comedian (b. 1915)
- November 29 – J. R. D. Tata, Indian aviator and businessman (b. 1904)

**December**

Frank Zappa

Don Ameche

Félix Houphouët-Boigny

Myrna Loy

- December 2 – Pablo Escobar, Colombian drug lord (b. 1949)
- December 3 – Lewis Thomas, American physician and essayist (b. 1913)
- December 4 – Frank Zappa, American guitarist and composer (b. 1940)
- December 5
    - Doug Hopkins, American musician (b. 1961)
    - Alexandre Trauner, Hungarian set designer (b. 1906)
- December 6
    - Don Ameche, American actor (b. 1908)
    - Joe Fowler, rear admiral of the United States Navy (b. 1894)
- December 7
    - Wolfgang Paul, German physicist, Nobel Prize laureate (b. 1913)

- o Félix Houphouët-Boigny, Ivorian president (b. 1905)
- December 9
  - o Danny Blanchflower, Northern Ireland international footballer and football manager (b. 1926)
  - o Mohammad-Reza Golpaygani, Iranian Shia cleric and marja (b. 1898)
- December 12
  - o József Antall, Hungarian Prime Minister (b. 1932)
  - o Fritz Bock, Austrian politician (b. 1911)
- December 13
  - o George Bellew, genealogist and armorist (b. 1899)
  - o Tommy Sexton, Canadian comedian (b. 1957)
- December 14 – Myrna Loy, American actress (b. 1905)
- December 15
  - o Evelyn Venable, American actress (b. 1913)
  - o Penaia Ganilau, Fijian president (b. 1918)
- December 16
  - o Charles Willard Moore, American architect (b. 1926)
  - o Kakuei Tanaka, former Japanese Prime Minister (b. 1918)
  - o Moses Gunn, American actor (b. 1929)
  - o Billy Morgan, English professional footballer (b. 1896)
- December 17 – Janet Margolin, American actress (b. 1943)
- December 18
  - o Charizma, American hip hop artist (b. 1973)
  - o Sam Wanamaker, American film director and actor (b. 1919)
- December 20 – Iichirō Hatoyama, Japanese politician and diplomat (b. 1918)
- December 22
  - o Don DeFore, American actor (b. 1917)
  - o Alexander Mackendrick, British-American film director (b. 1912)
- December 24
  - o Norman Vincent Peale, American preacher and writer (b. 1898)
  - o Yen Chia-kan, former Taiwanese president (b. 1905)
  - o Pierre Victor Auger, French physicist (b. 1899)

- December 25 – Princess Marie Adelheid of Lippe-Biesterfeld, daughter of Prince Rudolf of Lippe-Biesterfeld (b. 1895)
- December 26 – Dave Beck, American labor leader (b. 1894)
- December 28
  - William L. Shirer, American journalist and historian (b. 1904)
  - Howard Caine, American actor (b.1926)
- December 30 – Ira Stanphill, American gospel songwriter (born 1914)
- December 31
  - Brandon Teena, American transman (b. 1972)
  - İhsan Sabri Çağlayangil, Turkish politician and diplomat (b. 1908)
  - Zviad Gamsakhurdia, President of Georgia (b. 1939)

# Nobel Prizes

- Chemistry – Kary Mullis, Michael Smith
- Economics – Robert W. Fogel, Douglass North
- Literature – Toni Morrison
- Peace – Nelson Mandela and Frederik Willem de Klerk
- Physics – Russell Alan Hulse, Joseph Hooton Taylor, Jr.
- Physiology or Medicine – Richard J. Roberts, Phillip Allen Sharp

# In the News

**Ferry in Haiti sinks** - over 1000 die.

**Space Shuttle** Endeavour mission to repair an optical flaw in the Hubble Space Telescope.

**Buckingham Palace** opens its doors to the public.

**Ben Johnson**, is banned from athletics for life.

**Police** begin investigations of child abuse by Michael Jackson.

**Popular Films -** Jurassic Park, Mrs. Doubtfire, The Fugitive.

**Federal Agents** raid religious cult Waco, Texas.

**Islamic Fundamentalists** bomb World Trade Center.

**Russian Nuclear** Accident at Tomask 7.

**Ty Warner** USA launches the first Beanie Babies.

**Earthquake** centered on Killari, Maharashtra, India kills nearly 10,000 people.

**In the United Kingdom,** 11-year-olds Robert Thompson and Jon Venables are convicted of the child murder of 2-year-old **James** Bulger of Liverpool.